THE CELEBRANTS
and Other Poems

Elaine Feinstein

THE CELEBRANTS
and Other Poems

HUTCHINSON OF LONDON

Hutchinson & Co (Publishers) Ltd
3 Fitzroy Square, London W1

London Melbourne Sydney Auckland
Wellington Johannesburg Cape Town
and agencies throughout the world

First published 1973
© Elaine Feinstein 1973

This book has been
set in Monotype Bembo,
printed and bound in Great Britain by
William Clowes & Sons, Limited
London, Beccles and Colchester

ISBN 0 09 117660 3 (cased)
      0 09 117661 1 (paper)

Some of these poems have appeared in *The Times Literary Supplement, Poetry Review, The Humanist, The New Yorker, Caret, Antaeus, European Judaism, Modern Poetry in Translation, The Scotsman, The Listener* and *Sceptre Press*.

FOR ANTONY AND NICOLE WARD

Contents

THE CELEBRANTS

I

    Remember Melusine
morose spectre, whose own superstition once
    made a serpent of her: she was
bewitched   into a myth   by chance
    out of her housekeeping because
she was credulous, and so wandered in
    bands of the spell-bound until
she fell into encephalitic trance. And still
    to her believing company she slithered
in green skin to the last day of her life.

II

Might be anyone's cracked daughter
sozzled, or skewed of vision, lonely,
    in winter months invoking mutinous powers

    that pour like mercury out of the moon
into the waiting mind with its own glass-lined
pumice craters and stains of orange oxide,

    always the occult temptation, the erotic
world-flicker, shining in wet streets
like coal with streaks of mica, for

    the demons rise at the first oblique
longing, they rise up nocturnal and cruel, and
the neophyte becomes their stammering mouth,

breaks into joy without drugs
dangerous, cannibal, frenetic with
forbidden knowledge, in deaf violence.

Bitten with toxic spiders, women
dance themselves into exhaustion knowing
the spirits that they bear are hostile

and yet are proud to be a hostage to them,
as if their hallucinations could be
a last weapon against humiliation:

Listen to their song: as
servants of the tribe they now
enter the crisis of their terror

willing to free us from the same service,
but their song draws us after them and
some will follow   into their own unreason.

III
Trees, under wet trees, I am beckoned down to a river
that runs into land through a sink of sedge and rushes,
white trench gas, between roots galled with witches fungus
cut stumps, where bodies of bald dogs stir at the crunch
                                                  of my feet.

The mud and black leaves are frozen these last hours of the
year, I follow this sloping path downwards, like a lost sleeper, in
fear of finding the faces, and hearing the voices, of those
who came this way   by the black stub alder   and under

in frost against spindle shrubs, or wych Elm in tangles of
twigs, and who swim in the smoke on the stream and beneath
the rotting bridge, and float head-high in the dark evergreen
yews, and hang waiting in that poisonous foliage.

Through hoots of long-eared owl, gunshot, and cries of
mallard across the marsh, what I fear is to hear their voices;
those obdurate spirits, haunted and harrassed, who once
came down this route and laid waste their energies here

to become mares of god, crying, and singing epiphanies.
They offered their eyes and their entrails for the forest
spirits to fill them like swallow-tailed kites:
they bartered their lives and the air tastes of their drowning.

15

IV

In the last hour of the magus, then as now, marauding
    students went about selling horoscopes from
Lisbon to Lithuania, diseases also wandered freely
    as any demons: plague, syphilis, cholera.

The kitchens of sober doctors glittered with
    sulphur, they cast urine, read
propitious constellations and applied their
    ostrich feathers, viper fat, mummy powder.

In miniver fur, bald, with a
    sword in his pommel, tricky as any sorcerer,
Paracelsus often cured his patients,
    for which the burghers hounded him as Faustus,

because he treated the sword instead of the wound
    believing in the natural magic of
healing in the flesh, with herbs and metals
    he challenged the dominion of the stars.

For such heresy he was nearly hanged at
    Salzburg, driven out of Poland, and of
Prussia, and at the last, without any follower
    he left Switzerland

without shoes or bag or even a stick
   in token that his realm was
not of this world, and yet doubting
   what entrance he could have to any other.

v
And this knowledge enters even
   between the bodies of lovers, though
we share each other's vigil: that our arms

hold water only, salt as the sea
   we come from, a spongework of
acid chains, our innermost landscape

an arcane pulp of flexible
   chemistry; sinus, tubes,
follicles, cells that wander

from red marrow in the crevices
   of our long bones across
membranes, blood-stream, thymus,

and lymph nodes   to defend
   our separate skin-bound
unit of internal territory.

Give me your astrolabe and now tell me
     what doing or refusing kills
or how we will our bodies treachery.

VI
The red giant Antares is in Scorpio;
     in fen fields a radio dish listens.
Who will give us a horoscope for the planet?
     On December 3 which is the Day of the Emigrant,

for those who come of the ancient tribe of Habiru
     nomads, wilderness people, having no
house of their own, or magicians; my desert
     grandmother laughed at the time to come.

Since then her daughters have seen Babylon
     Persepolis, Delphi, settled in Toledo
risen, and been flung over
     the north coast of Africa as Marranos.

From Clermont, the hill of the first Crusade
     we learnt things could be good only so long.
Our poets wrote that halls in heaven opened
     only to the voice of song, but their

boldest praise was always for
　　the holy stamina of body and spirit as one
which is the only sacrament will stand to
　　cold, fatigue, waiting, and starvation.

VII
Lonely as a hangman through
　　sweet mustard streets, at seventy
being sad and wily and austere

Buonarotti worked in fear
　　for his soul, living
in prudence and squalor.

For our wood dries out,
　　we shall not be
green again. In all

the bull-strong beauties of
　　his torso he let in
the pressure of death,

he made it known, and
　　in his dead Christ also
the full weight of strength

in a dead man. Yet where
   is the protection of
the broken body put under the ground?

VIII
Fear the millennial cities
   jasper-lit, descending
with oil and wine and corn
   from ancient prophecies,

where men with lidless eyes
   through centuries will slither
in holy crystal streets
   on the blood of massacre.

Their secret flagellant rites
   and luminous scars declare
a godhead and release
   for any follower,

but every incarnation, from
   Schmidt of Thuringia, to
the lost of our Los Angeles
   reveals itself in murder.

And only the bitch leader
   of a Jenghis pack can show
a spite   as human   as adepts
   of those who call Messiah.

IX
Today the air is cold and bitter as kale
   the sky porcelaine, the sun bleached
to white metal: I am alight with ions

awake   alert   under
   that ancient primal blue, which is
the serene accident of our atmosphere;

tethered by winter gold in
   the hair of these
bare willows on my own green waterside.

Here birds and poets may
   sing for their time
without intrusion from

either priest or physician;
   for the Lord relents; he is
faithful. In his silence.

Having no sound or name
  he cannot be conjured.
All his greatness is in this:

to free us from the
  black drama
of the magician.

OTHER POEMS

Chance

Pink and shining as a scatter of lentils
    in my sleep my broken trellis
blossomed this morning with a freak tamarisk:
    it seems my town soil has its prodigies

that cannot be willed, cannot be sown, and flourish
    in what is tired and pale but yet not seedless
as if even decay could be generous, and only
    the gardened stone fail to astonish.

Love Song

In fluorescent white
   across a glacial sky
a weightless winter lights
   your scorched and sleepless eye

and thoughts like frozen rain, in
   brittle splinters fall
like glass into my brain,
   to spike my stubborn core.

So often at its bleakest
   your vision conquers mine,
yet quietly and quietly
   my spirits thaw again:

wet streetlights shine this
   morning, a line of minarets,
and mad quince buds on our north wall
   exact our stunned respect.

The Medium

My answer would have to be music
which is always deniable, since in my
silence, which you question, is only a landscape

of water, old trees and a few irresolute
birds. The weather is also inconstant.
Sometimes the light is golden, the leaves unseasonable.

And sometimes the ice is red, and the moon
hangs over it, peeled, like a chinese fruit.
I am sorry not to be more articulate.

When I try, the words turn ugly as rats and
disorder everything, I cannot be quiet,
I want so much to be quiet and loving

If only you wanted that. My sharpest thoughts
wait like assassins always in the dry wheat. They
chat and grin. Perhaps you should talk to them?

Night thoughts

Uncurtained, my long room floats on
    darkness, moored in rain,
my shelves of orange skillets
    lie out in the black grass.
Tonight I can already taste
    the wet soil of their ghosts.
And my spirit looks through the glass:
    I cannot hold on for ever.

No tenure, in garden trees, I
    hang like a leaf, and stare
at cartilaginous shapes
    my shadow their visitor.
And words cannot brazen it out.
    Nothing can hold for ever.

'The only good life is lived without miracles'. (N. Mandelstam)

Under hot white skies, if we could,
in this city of bridges and pink stone live gratefully
here is a lacework of wooden ghosts from New Guinea
Etruscan jewels, beetles with scales of blue mineral.

Bad news follows us, however. I wonder if
anyone walks sanely in middle age. Isn't there
always some desperation for the taste of one last
miraculous fruit, that has to be pulled from the air?

Nachtfest

Water black water at night the Rhine and
in small boats lanterns like
coloured souls solemnly passing

into darkness, into circles of silver, into
black quick currents of water hidden as
the trees that rise over us steeply

up to the pink stone of the Munster, floating in
floodlight, Erasmus lies there lost, the leaves of
green and gold tile are shining,

fountains of white fire pour down the living
cliffs of pine, over drinking Baselers, a
mist of flies

gathers around the bulbs of the
bandstand. Now on a darkened raft held by ropes invisibly
in the centre of the river

men prepare the festival rockets, when
in spasms of red and green those sticks shoot
into the sky, their

light draws our breath upwards, we are gone
over the low moon after them into a
black imagination of depth more final than water.

The Sources

And how to praise them? Through the bad teeth of Europe
                                                    we had
   tasted the breath of the Bruges canals, between old
houses, water and lichen ate into us;
   and we had slept by the waters of Köln, where
detergent fluff rises every morning from the river at sunlight.

Yet the sources are not gentle. Through the wet brown caves of
   Trümmelbach, there is a ceaseless rush of water, one solid
thrust through the mountain, listen, in that sound is the whole
   force of the planet. Yes, delicate under the
trees, quietly over stones to rock pools, shining
   between grass, sometimes in a
long slow fall of fine spray vanishing or in rain
   a smell of the soil in a night of blue lightning.
The true beauty of fall is fierce. Drenched and shaking
   what frail homage to so brutal a purity?

A year gone

Who believes
he is dead?
in the ground
that lies over his head
in the rain, under leaves, in the earth
who believes he is
there?

In the tick
of our blood
in the blue
muscles under our tongue
in our skulls
where a hidden ice-pick may be waiting
we must
learn

how at last
motionless
we shall fall without
breath into place

and the pain of our questions will melt like the
wax of our flesh
into silence.

A September friend

Through your erotic landscape lit with tallow flares
grotesque and valiant lady of red eyes
you move as slowly as a boat dragged overland:
while lamed and sleepless creatures hop
after you, or fall out of your skirt.

With lonely stamina you spin the
necessary thread to hide your movements.
Why should we try to judge
your true direction? Fluently
as the grass darkens and the rain begins to
fall through sulphurous trees like strings of glass

iron wheels will roll us all underground.
Their growl is in my ears, even as I
now call up the last of your shifting images
with sadness: for you bear yourself bravely.

A ritual turning

(For Octavio Paz)

They shall be black metal and bone now those
treacherous and beautiful covens, tonight
I am burning a pyre of ash and
lime boughs in my heart to rid of them,
those fingers beckoning, their
offer sweet mud in the mouth
damp, illicit. No-one who
listens to that song is satisfied
until he breathes in the deathly
tars of the same intoxication.
Now I know
a man can sing with only an erotic stammer to
mark the white line of his transgression: birds
golden as weeds by the waterside return, their
delicate feet step upon green stone.
For the earth has another language, we have been
given complexities of the soil against the taste of the grave.

At the Edge

In your delirium your eyelids were
    raisin brown, and your beard like wet straw.
We were washed in salt on the same pillow together
    and we watched the walls change level gently as water.

But now there are white drops at the window
    this morning, in grey light, your fever gone,
do you even remember the dance of words that
    slipped between us like fish? My sober love.

II
Behind your darkness and
marooned again: I know that
island, sisters, where you wait to
offer your magenta crenellations
to some explorer, unafraid of the moon.

Yet I would bless you with no
causewayside, no mainland even,
but only more silence for you to turn in
so you receive at last whatever
light your creole petals need to open.

III

Into sleet over
stones and shells
on a visit to Winchelsea
to that lake of wet sand and sky where
the red water runs
salt from
sun into sea,

we laughed
crunching over
snow pouches to leap
at the planet's periphery
but our cries
died about us:

we were
black points upon
too inhuman a canvas
and were dwindling fast.
It was not just the Ural wind
drove us
inland for shelter.

Mas-en-Cruyes

Once
in the white powdered earth of
Provence, where the fire-winds
blow hillsides of pinebranch to ash
in your barn
where you fed us
thrush paté and wine

We were friends:
we drank fish-soup and Pastis
alongside Cassis; in a feckless alliance
of the gross
and tenacious. I cannot remember
why we fought to be free.

But I offer
this song now, for the days lived in peace
in the twentyfour houses we've shared,
and the beauties of August,
the dry wind of Provence, and
the shelter you gave us
once   in Mas-en-Cruyes.

Survivors

In these miraculous Catalan streets, yellow
as falling barberry, and urine-scented, the
poorest Jews of Rome are at every orifice,

those that remain, the centuries have
left moneyless, and the new Romans
drive past them with a blank polaroid stare.

Even in the Synagogue their service
goes on separately in a cellar
because they came through Fez once, not directly

out of Spain. Whatever happened then
their latest dead sit in gold letters
with the rest. All that is puzzling to understand

is what the power could be that brings them out
on Friday night, after so many lessons
to laugh in garrulous Sabbath on this pavement?

Green

In the resonance of that
lizard colour, mottled like stone from
Eilat, with blue fruit and patches
of mud in it: my thoughts scatter

over Europe where there is water
and sunlight in collision, and green is
the flesh of Holbein's coffined Christ, and
also the liturgical colour of heaven.

In England: green is innocent as grass.

Free Will

Once in a dream a graph was already
   prepared for the moment of my death:
I was present, but my flesh was
   already yellow and stiffening, I could
hardly refuse the line's black evidence.

—But who is it? I demanded: Who can lay
   a claim to so much prescience? And then
as soon as I understood the name of the enemy,
   I sprang up out of my sleep to resist.

For who knows when, or what dangerous bodily
   mechanism may be triggered by
my own concealed and cavernous treachery?

Lais

Lais, courtesan of Corinth, why has
Holbein given you so mild a face,
and why now does your gentle hand lie open
beside those golden coins you do not take?

Sad mother and serious, your service
must be in some way most benevolent,
a holy trimmer in this Protestant city:
you cannot hide the evidence of grace.

November songs

I

The air is rising tonight and the leaf dust is
   burning in cadmium bars, the skinny beeches
are alight in the town fire of their own humus.
   There is oxblood in the sky. No month to be surly.

The attic cracks and clicks as we ride the night
   our bodies spiced with salt and olive sweetness:
but a savoury smoke is hanging in our hair,
   for the earth turns, and the air of the earth rises.

And it blows November spores over the sash.
   The sky is a red lichen in the mirror,
as the air rises we already breathe in the
   oracular resins of the season.

II

And now what aureole possesses the fine
   extremities of my leafless trees? They are
Florentine today, their fen wood is ochre

an afternoon's bewildering last
   sunlight honours their sunken
life with an alien radiance:

and we, who are restless by the
    same accident that gives their
vegetable patience   grace

may worship the tranquillity of
    waiting, but will not
find such blessing in the human face.

Newspaper elegy

The cold that killed Patel
last Tuesday in the Park
by the rubbish tip
where he fell, was
nothing unnatural:

to be hungry, thin, eleven
and sit in a wet anorak
after falling in a lake
was dangerous. And our English
November air can be murderous.

Sybil

The present holder of the papers sits
behind broken glass in the derelict warehouse
androgynous, black-skulled, and ricket-boned
grimacing to deride her visitors,

skinny, tobacco-stained, alert, she has
bartered her memories of
bark smells, wild
almonds and water plants to
taste the sour air of neglected cities.

Trembling with adrenalin of
indignation, like euphoria, she
licks her lips at the modern
crystal set in the wall. Look,

it is all happening again.
We can watch together
how terror smiles through the screen
like a handsome peasant with his violin.

She sits and nods and waits for
the latest obsequies, with
a squint eye and a slant hand, she
writes: beware this generation's prophecies.

In bed

Between rose quartz and sea-cabbage this morning
   the postman tacked towards me through
my dreams, I could hear the
   hiss of his cycle wheel approaching

but huddled deeper into my sea-bed
   to hide among the other marine creatures;
knowing envelopes below could hold
   ugly surprises in their brown manilla.

The first Siren

And I must go back:
along a canal where the water
is the colour of the plum, and the sky between
crimson and lavender.
I must walk,
not run.

The zoo has entered the town. First
the blue-lipped rhino, then
the gross bear. I can already hear
the cry of the wild cats.
All these years their cages
have been frail as solder.

The guns are waiting
now, loaded with valium.
Whose side are you on?
My friends, will you take arms
against the days to come?

From The Shrews of the Sea

(From the French of Louis René des Forêts)

Time to return, and my fever it is carries me to the
furthest edge of the shore-line to find some shelter;
slant as a hooked fish I am already moving now with
sea-weed on my head for a crown, on fire, I rush to
prick the red-brown fog of a late spring.
My feet rasp over that grating mosaic of the seas'
wreckage, there are knife-shells, blue as jays, dead starfish
and verminous excrement, potsherds with cutting edges, I am
no more than a beast that groans as it is taken,
and my throat is torn with an exhausting scream:
terror is sharp, and the wind also, yet
nothing diverts the pure line of my trajectory,
not deep pockets of squirting water, nor some bushy stump
against my naked limbs, that bristles like a hedgehog of ivory.
If I take breath again, it is only to climb
the slope where from the saddle of a rock spur
I see under the porch of my hand, guided by
fetid effluvia, like six sapless trees, white-haired
gorgons against a fog of fire, etching their twin
profiles into the bodies of tubers: they are
Egyptian mummies of these caves, dressed in their
own shadows, in silvery mist, their hands waving.
Some dark fury has driven you wild, you slobbering
Medusas, so you throw sprays of madness against the wind!
And I, who was kept so pure by the laughter of childhood
once, I was a proud boy, nothing could bend me,
but they have stolen my freedom to draw me into

their lair, if I close my eyes it is always
their voices I hear, and their bitter wish to damage me
is there in the sweetness of their invitations.
Understand, my own slim glory is extinct now, yet
this uncouth citadel was once the only theatre
of my passion, I suffer now in memory which is
my last possession, as I look within it for
any mark the child I was might have left.

Song

(From the Russian of Marina Tsvetayeva)

Yesterday he still looked in my eyes, yet
    today   his looks are bent aside. Yesterday
he sat here until the birds began, but
    today   all those larks are   ravens.

Stupid creature! And you are wise, you
    live while I am stunned.
Now for the lament of women in all times:
    —My love, what was it I did to you?

And tears are   water, blood is   water,
    a woman always washes in blood and tears.
Love is a step-mother, and no mother:
    then expect no justice or mercy from her.

Ships carry away the ones we love.
    Along the white road they are taken away.
And one cry stretches across the earth:
    —My love, what was it I did to you?

Yesterday he lay at my feet. He even
    compared me with the Chinese empire! Then
suddenly he let his hands fall open, and
    my life fell out like   a rusty kopeck.

A child-murderer, before some court
    I stand   loathsome and timid I am.
And yet even in Hell I shall demand:
    —My love, what was it I did to you?

I ask this chair, I ask the bed: Why?
    Why do I suffer and live in penury?
His kisses stopped. He wanted to break you.
    To kiss another girl is their reply.

He taught me to live in fire, he threw me there,
    and then abandoned me on steppes of ice.
My love, I know what you have done to me.
    —My love, what was it I did to you?

I know everything, don't argue with me!
    I can see now, I'm a lover no longer.
And now I know wherever love hold power
    Death approaches soon   like a gardener.

It is almost like shaking a tree, in time
    some ripe apple comes falling down. So
for everything, for everything   forgive me,
    my love   whatever it was I did to you.

Fever

(From the Russian of Bella Akhmadulina)

I must be ill, of course. I've been shivering
for three days now like a horse before the races.
Even the haughty man who lives on my landing
has said as much to me:
Bella, you're shaking!

Please control yourself, this strange disease of yours
is rocking the walls, it gets in everywhere.
My children are driven mad by it, and at night
it shatters all my cups and kitchenware.

I tried to answer him: Yes,
I do tremble,
more and more, though I mean no harm to anyone.
But tell everyone on the floor, in any case,
I've made up my mind to leave the house this evening.

However, I was then so jerked about by
fever, my words shook with it; my legs
wobbled; I couldn't even bring my
lips together into the shape of a smile.

My neighbour, leaning over the bannister,
observed me with disgust he didn't hide.
Which I encouraged.
—This is just
a beginning. What happens next, I wonder.

Because this is no ordinary illness. I'm sorry to
tell you, there are as many wild and
alien creatures flashing about in me
as in a drop of water under a microscope.

My fever lashed me harder and harder, and
drove its sharp nails under my skin. It was
something like the rain whipping an
aspen tree, and damaging every leaf.

I thought: I seem to be moving about rapidly
as I stand here, at least my muscles are moving.
My body is out of my control completely.
The thing is freely doing whatever it likes.

And it's getting away from me. I wonder if
it will suddenly and dangerously disappear?
Like a ball slipping out of a child's hand,
or a piece of string unreeling from a finger?

I didn't like any of it. To
the doctor
I said, (though I'm timid with him)
—You know, I'm a proud woman! I can't have my
body disobeying me for ever!

My doctor explained:
Yours is a simple disease,
perhaps even harmless, unfortunately
you are vibrating so fast I can't examine you.

You see, when anything vibrates, as you are,
and its movements are so very quick and small,
the object is reduced, visibly speaking
to—nothing. All I can see is: mist.

So my doctor put his golden instrument
against my indefinite body, and a sharp
electric wave chilled me at once
as if I had been flooded with green fire

and the needle and the scales registered horror.
The mercury began to seethe with violence.
The glass shattered, everything splashed about,
and a few splinters drew blood from my fingers.

—Be careful, doctor, I cried. But
he wasn't worried.
Instead, he proclaimed: Your
poor organism is
now functioning normally.

Which made me sad. I knew myself to belong
to another norm than he had ever intended.
One that floated above my own spirit only
because I was too narrow for such immensity.

And those many figures of my ordeals had
trained my nervous system so that now
my nerves were bursting through my skin, like old
springs through a mattress, screeching at me.

My wrist was still out of shape with its huge
and buzzing pulse, that always had insisted
on racing freely: Damn it, run free then, I cried
I'll choke with you, as Neva chokes St Petersburg.

For at night my brain has become so sharp with
waiting, my ear opens to silence, if
a door squeaks or a book drops, then—
with an explosion—it's the end of me.

I have never learnt to tame those beasts
inside, that guzzle human blood.
In my presence, draughts blow under doors!
Candles flare—before I extinguish them!

And one enormous tear is always ready
to spill over the rim of my eyes.
My own spirit distorts everything.
I have a hell inside would corrupt heaven.

The doctor wrote me out a Latin scrip.
The sensible and healthy girl in
the chemist shop was able to read
the music in it from the punctuation.

And now my whole house has been softened by
the healing kiss of that valerian,
the medicine has licked into every
wound I have, with its minty tongue.

My neighbour is delighted, three times he
has congratulated me on my recovery,
(through his children). He has even
put a word in for me with the house management.

I have repaid a few visits and debts already,
answered some letters. I wander about
in some kind of profitable circles.
And no longer keep any wine in my cupboard.

Around me—not a sound, not a soul.
My table is dead, dust hides everything on it.
My blunt pencils like illiterate
snouts, are all lying in darkness.

And like a defeated horse, all my
steps are sluggish and hobbling now.
So all is well. But my nights are
disturbed with certain dangerous premonitions.

My doctor has not yet found me out. However
it will not long be possible to
fool him. He may have cured me once, but
soon I know I shall burn and freeze again.

A snail in its grave of bone, I am
for the moment saved by blindness and silence—
but still the horns of sick antennae itch
and will rise up once again from my forehead.

Star-fall of full stops and hyphens, I
summon your shower to me! I want to
die with the silvery goose-flesh of
water nymphs burning in my spine.

Fever! I am your tambourine, strike me
without pity! I shall dance, like
a ballerina to your music, or
live like a chilled puppy in your frost.

So far I haven't even begun to
shiver. No, let's not even discuss that. Yet
my observant neighbour is already
becoming rather cold to me when we meet.